Cornerstones of Freedom

Reconstruction

BRENDAN JANUARY

CHILDREN'S PRESS®
A Division of Grolier Publishing
New York • London • Hong Kong • Sydney
Danbury, Connecticut

Visit Children's Press on the Internet at:
http://publishing.grolier.com

Library of Congress Cataloging-in-Publication Data

January, Brendan, 1972–
    Reconstruction / Brendan January.
        p. cm.— (Cornerstones of freedom)
    Includes index.
    Summary: A history of Reconstruction, the period after the Civil War
during which programs were implemented to bring the Confederate States
back to the Union.
    ISBN: 0-516-21143-9 (lib. bdg.)   0-516-26461-3 (pbk.)
    1. Reconstruction—Juvenile literature. [1. Reconstruction.]
I. Title. II. Series.
E668.J38 1999
973.8—dc21
                                                                    98-3492
                                                                        CIP
                                                                        AC

During spring 1865, the American Civil War was coming to a close. General Robert E. Lee's Confederate (Southern) army marched westward into central Virginia. The soldiers were exhausted and hungry. The hills and roads around the battered Confederates were filled with pursuing Union (Northern) soldiers. Every day, they attacked the Confederates, capturing thousands of prisoners. On April 8, General Lee sent a message to the Union general, Ulysses S. Grant. The two men met the next day, and Lee surrendered his army.

Robert E. Lee signed surrender papers, as Union General Ulysses S. Grant looked on, in a farmhouse at Appomattox Court House, Virginia, on April 9, 1865.

The Civil War had started more than four years earlier, when a group of southern states led by South Carolina seceded from, or left, the Union. The southern states wanted to form their own country where they could freely practice slavery. In the North, many people argued that slavery was immoral and cruel. Southerners insisted that slavery was their right.

In February 1861, the seceding states formed their own country, called the Confederate States of America. On April 14, 1861, Confederate forces bombarded the Union's Fort Sumter in Charleston Harbor, South Carolina. President Abraham Lincoln called for a volunteer army to crush the southern rebellion. Thousands responded, and the Civil War began.

The American Civil War divided the United States. (Border states were slave-holding states that did not secede.)

Free states
Slave states
Border states

During the first year of the war, the Confederates defeated a Union army in northern Virginia. The North's hopes for a short war were dashed. The war dragged on, and Union armies began advancing into the South and capturing Confederate land. The captured land sparked a debate in the North. How would these areas become a part of the Union again? Some members of Congress argued that the Confederates should be severely punished before any area could reenter the Union. Lincoln, however, did not favor harsh measures. Wanting to reunite the country as quickly as possible, he developed a plan—Reconstruction.

As the Civil War continued, soldiers such as these in the Union Army, filled their time in camp by writing letters and mending uniforms.

Abraham Lincoln

President Lincoln's plan was simple. In Union-occupied Confederate territory, he required that ten percent of the region's population swear loyalty to the United States government. When that number was reached, representatives could then be sent to Congress. Once the congressmen were seated in Washington, D.C., the area's reentry into the Union would be complete.

Many northern congressmen, however, were outraged. They believed Lincoln's plan made it too easy for the southerners to rejoin the Union. Too many Union soldiers had died, they argued, and change was needed throughout the South. One northern congressman expressed his disgust, "The people of the North are not such fools as to fight through such a war as this . . . and then turn around and say to the traitors, 'all you have to do is to come back . . . and take an oath.' " To make matters worse, Lincoln had avoided taking any advice from Congress on how to achieve Reconstruction. Insulted and angry at being ignored by the president, northern congressmen created their own plan for Reconstruction in 1864.

Congress's program was far more strict than Lincoln's. To rejoin the Union, more than half of a territory's population had to take an oath of loyalty. Lincoln did not approve of the plan, and he refused to sign it into law.

As the president and Congress argued, a new problem emerged. In 1863, Lincoln had issued the Emancipation Proclamation, which freed the slaves in the Confederate states. By 1865, Union armies, deep in the South, reported that thousands of slaves were running away from their owners. Northern generals sent urgent letters to Washington requesting orders. They did not know what to do with the former slaves, or "freedmen," as they were now called. Most of the freedmen owned little or no property, and few of them could read or write. Congress responded by forming the Freedmen's Bureau in March 1865 to help freedmen adjust to their new freedom. By the time the war ended, the bureau had opened offices throughout the South. It began giving out food, clothing, and medicine.

After the Emancipation Proclamation was issued in 1863, slaves throughout the South who could not wait for the outcome of the war escaped from their owners.

By war's end, plantations throughout the South, many of which had been the sites of fighting, were destroyed.

In late spring 1865, southern whites looked in despair at the ruin caused by four years of war. Blackened stumps of chimneys were all that remained of once-magnificent mansions. Industrial machines lay smashed and useless. Farm fields were choked with weeds. One reporter described the South as "a desolated land. Every village we stopped at presented ruined walls and chimneys standing useless." Stunned Confederate soldiers returned to their shattered homes. A Confederate general wrote: "My shoes are gone, my clothes are almost gone. I'm sick. I'm weary. My family have been killed or scattered." White southerners were angry and resentful. And they had no desire to treat former slaves as equals.

Houston Holloway felt differently about the Confederate defeat. Holloway was a twenty-year-old black slave freed by the Union victory. He described the new feeling of freedom: "I felt like a bird out of a cage. Amen. Amen. Amen. I could hardly ask to feel any better than I did on that day." Close to four million slaves were freed at the end of the war. They quickly embraced the joy of freedom. They became legally married, searched for lost loved ones, and began to plan for the future. They looked forward to owning their own land and enjoying the rights guaranteed to all American citizens.

Their hopes turned to sorrow when Abraham Lincoln was shot at Ford's Theatre on April 14, 1865. Lincoln clung to life through that night, but died early the next day. The nation bitterly mourned its loss. Vice President Andrew Johnson, was immediately sworn in as the new president. Throughout the country, people wondered what kind of leader the new president would be.

John Wilkes Booth shot Lincoln in the head as the president enjoyed a play with his wife Mary and two other guests.

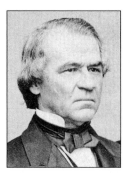

Andrew Johnson

Johnson had originally served as a southern congressman from Tennessee. When Tennessee joined the Confederacy in 1860, Johnson was the only southern representative to reject secession. He refused to give up his seat in Congress, even though all the seats around him were empty. Johnson blamed the war on wealthy southerners who owned large plantations and most of the South's slaves. Poor white southerners, Johnson believed, had been tricked by the wealthy southerners into fighting a ruinous war.

Johnson's support for the Union made him a hero throughout the North. After Tennessee was occupied by the Union army in 1863, Lincoln appointed Johnson governor of Tennessee. He served bravely in the post and established a pro-Union government. In 1864, Lincoln asked Johnson to be his vice president. Johnson agreed. But eight months after winning the presidential election, Lincoln was dead. Johnson suddenly found himself leading a country whose people desperately needed healing from the horrors of war and the assassination of a president.

At first, many northerners were pleased with President Johnson. He was a Republican, and he had attacked southern slave owners in his fiery speeches. "Traitors [to the Union] must be punished and impoverished," he once stated. But though Johnson despised rich white southerners, he did not favor equal rights for blacks. He believed that "white men alone must manage the South."

This attitude angered and worried many northerners. In Congress, a group called the Radical Republicans believed that blacks should be given the right to vote and to own land. These congressmen watched in alarm as Johnson continued Lincoln's lenient plan of Reconstruction. In summer 1865, Johnson pardoned hundreds of former Confederates and called for elections throughout the South. Only whites were allowed to vote. Quickly, new southern state governments were elected. Johnson made only a few requirements for the new state governments to reenter the Union. The most important of these were: declaring secession illegal and passing the Thirteenth Amendment to the Constitution, which abolished slavery forever.

This famous depiction of former slaves as victims of the white men who ruled the government appeared in Harper's Weekly.

11

Johnson's plan pleased southerners who wanted to rejoin the Union. But the Radical Republicans grew more concerned. After the elections, former Confederates took control in the South. They began passing laws, called Black Codes, to return freedmen to slavery.

Black Codes stripped the freedmen of their civil rights. Freedmen were not allowed to vote or to hold office. To travel, they had to receive permission from their white employer. If a black person wanted to work as anything other than a farmer, he or she had to receive permission from a white judge.

This rioting took place in Memphis, Tennessee, in 1866.

In addition to the Black Codes, a rising tide of violence swept through the South. Wherever freedmen demonstrated their pride or enthusiasm for freedom, whites attacked and sometimes murdered them. An observer in Louisiana noted that whites "govern by the pistol and the rifle." An ex-slave named Henry Adams wrote, "I saw white men whipping colored men just the same as they did before the war." Shocking reports of violence and racism drifted north.

Northerners watched these developments with growing alarm. Their hope for a peaceful and quick Reconstruction faded. Disturbingly, most southerners showed little regret about the war. The new southern state governments refused to admit that secession was wrong. In Mississippi, voters even failed to ratify the Thirteenth Amendment. Northerners were stunned. An observer wrote that northerners believed "that somehow the South had never really surrendered after all."

When northern congressmen reassembled in Washington, D.C., in December 1865, they were in a foul mood. The newspapers were filled with reports of murder and violence in the South. To make matters worse, newly elected representatives arrived from the southern states. Many of these representatives had served in the Confederate government and army.

Alexander H. Stephens, who had served as the vice president of the Confederacy, was elected to Congress in 1866.

After four years of bloody warfare, Congress refused to allow elected southerners to take their seats. Some congressmen severely criticized Johnson for abandoning the freedmen. Enraged by Congress, Johnson demanded that the southern representatives be seated. Reconstruction, he claimed, was over. Instead, Congress investigated Johnson's program of Reconstruction and declared that it had failed. Throughout the South, the freedmen were being returned to slavery. Something had to be done.

Despite the controversy over Reconstruction, the Freedmen's Bureau continued to provide food and supplies to blacks in the South.

The Freedmen's Bureau continued to provide aid to blacks throughout the South. It established schools and hospitals. In February 1866, Congress gave the bureau more power to defend freedmen against the Black Codes. The congressmen wrote

these measures into a bill and sent it to Johnson for approval.

President Johnson vetoed the Freedmen's Bill. Each state, Johnson insisted, has the Constitutional right to determine the laws within its own borders. The federal government in Washington, D.C., could not order state citizens around.

Congress was stunned by Johnson's veto. "The President has gone over to the enemy," wrote one Republican congressman bitterly. In March, Congress passed a second bill, called the Civil Rights Act. The bill gave freedmen civil rights and promised to protect them. Again, Johnson vetoed the bill. This time, Congress had enough votes to override Johnson's veto and the Civil Rights Act became law. Johnson angrily addressed a crowd at the White House after hearing the news. He claimed that Congress was filled with traitors.

Johnson's remarks lost him his support in Congress and shocked the North. The Radical Republicans now saw an opportunity. During the winter of 1866–67, they created a plan of Reconstruction to replace Johnson's. Their ideas were bold and revolutionary. The Radical Republicans wanted to guarantee civil rights to the freedmen. They saw Reconstruction as a chance to create a society where all men were truly "created equal," as stated in the Declaration of Independence.

Thaddeus Stevens, a leader of the Radical Republicans, summarized the ideas of his party:

Thaddeus Stevens

"Every man, no matter what his race or color . . . has an equal right to justice, honesty, and fair play with every other man; and the law should secure him those rights. . . . Such is the law of God and such ought to be the law of man."

To guarantee the freedmen's rights, Congress passed a new amendment to the Constitution— the Fourteenth—in June 1866. The amendment gave all citizens, including blacks, protection of their civil rights. It was then sent to the states to be approved. The amendment widened the gulf between Johnson and Congress. He publicly attacked it. Encouraged by Johnson, all of the former Confederate states (except Tennessee), Delaware, and Kentucky rejected the amendment.

Worse, ugly incidents of violence continued to rock the South. In July, blacks demonstrated in New Orleans, Louisiana, for the right to vote. A mob of white policemen and firemen brutally attacked them. By the time the clash ended, forty-eight people, mostly black, had been killed. After reading these reports, people across the North sided with the freedmen. A white man from Rhode Island wrote to Congress asking "that our country do something to repay the immense debt we owe them [the freedmen]. I cannot but feel that it was their prayers and strong arms that helped save our Union in the hour of deepest peril."

In November 1866, northern voters gave the Republicans a crushing victory in Congress. Backed by northern opinion, the Radical Republicans launched a new program called Radical Reconstruction. Thaddeus Stevens stated: "The whole fabric of southern society must be changed." On March 2, 1867, Congress passed the First Reconstruction Act. The act disbanded all southern state governments. The former Confederacy was divided into five districts, each ruled by a military governor who was appointed by Congress. New state elections were called. This time, ex-Confederates were not allowed to vote. To protect the freedmen and to keep order, columns of Union soldiers marched into the South.

By the middle of 1867, the South was divided into five military districts.

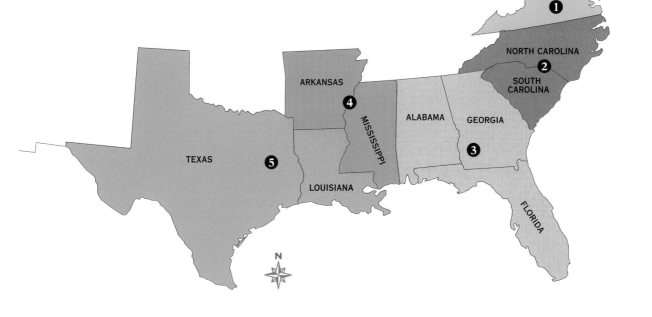

18

Proud and defiant, the freedmen came out to vote for the first time. An observer recorded that blacks "voted their entire walking strength—no one staying at home who could come to the polls." Southern whites reacted to these developments with fury. One man wrote: "I think most gentlemen felt as I did, that the negroes voting at all was . . . wicked."

Throughout the South, freedmen held political gatherings to discuss how they would vote for certain issues.

With Republicans in charge, southern society was turned upside down. Sixteen blacks were elected to the United States Congress. Free blacks and former slaves took seats next to whites in southern state governments. Despite bitter resistance from many whites, the new governments swiftly enacted reforms. They established the first public school systems in the South, benefiting both whites and blacks. Imprisonment for debts was ended. Taxes were spread out more evenly among the rich and the poor. Volunteers arrived from the North to help teach the freedmen to read and write. The schools were soon flooded with eager students.

A northern schoolteacher helps her students in Beaufort, South Carolina, in 1866. Freedmen's Bureau officials there reported that "the children were eager for knowledge."

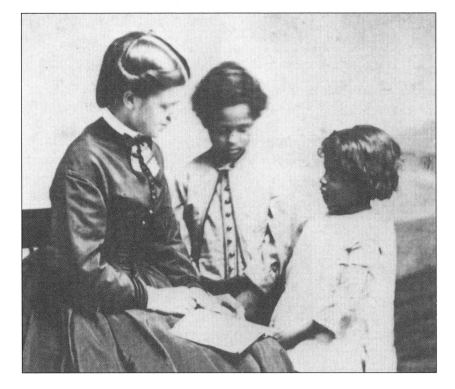

Blacks organized throughout the South. They demanded higher pay for their work. They insisted on being granted their civil rights. One southerner wrote: "You never saw a people more excited on the subject of politics than are the blacks of the south."

Thousands of northern whites also settled in the South. Amidst the crumbling ruins of war, they saw an opportunity for new industry and growth. They opened mines, built factories, and replanted crops such as cotton and tobacco. Slowly, the South was rebuilt. Most southern whites bitterly resented the "Yankee invaders." The southerners called them carpetbaggers because they often arrived from the North with their belongings in a carpetbag. Southerners claimed that carpetbaggers made money off of the misery of the South. Any southern white who worked with the carpetbaggers was labeled a scalawag, or traitor.

Carpetbaggers were depicted as greedy business-men who took advantage of southerners.

Dominated by blacks and whites who supported Radical Reconstruction, the southern states reentered the Union. Arkansas, Alabama, Florida, Louisiana, North Carolina, and South Carolina all accepted the Fourteenth Amendment and were readmitted in 1868.

In Congress, Radical Republican Charles Sumner urged the national government to do more. He suggested that giant plantations be broken up and the land divided among the freedmen. However, one congressmen protested, "That is more than we do for white men."

"White men have never been in slavery!" Sumner thundered back. Despite his efforts, Sumner's bold idea did not become law. In the South, land was returned to the wealthy planters who had owned it before the Civil War. Poor blacks and whites were forced to become sharecroppers. A share-cropper rented a piece of land by surrendering part of his crop as payment. But several years of crop failure crippled the South after the Civil War.

In this idealized version, Reconstruction is depicted as a woman who binds the Southern states back into the Union.

Sharecroppers could not pay their rents and many went deeply into debt. The freedmen's dream to farm their own land was shattered.

As the southern economy grew worse, white southerners blamed Reconstruction and the new state governments. Union troops became the object of resentment and anger. A new organization of hatred and violence, called the Ku Klux Klan (KKK), arose in the South. The KKK wanted to drive out the Republicans, return blacks to a state of slavery, and return southern whites to power. To achieve this, they began attacking local Republican government officials. KKK members dressed in white robes and masks to conceal their identity. Often traveling at night, they terrorized any black who dared to vote Republican.

An 1868 photograph of two Alabama members of the Ku Klux Klan in their disguises

In Washington, D.C., President Johnson resisted desperately as Congress carried out its plan for Reconstruction. One observer described Johnson, "He attempts to govern after he has lost the means to govern. He is like a general fighting without an army." In spring 1868, Congress launched a campaign to have Johnson impeached (removed from office). After a month of arguing and debating, Johnson's presidency barely survived—by one vote. In November 1868, former Union General Ulysses S. Grant was elected the eighteenth president of the

The U.S. Senate during the 1868 impeachment trial of President Andrew Johnson

United States. The Radical Republicans rejoiced. Grant took office with the slogan, "Let us have peace."

Ulysses S. Grant

Despite Grant's election, the Republican plan for Reconstruction began to meet resistance throughout the North. Although most northerners supported black civil rights in the South, they were slow to practice these rights in their own states. In the North, blacks were often a despised group with few rights. Surprisingly, Reconstruction had given blacks in the South more freedom than blacks in the North. The journal *Independent* wrote that northerners should be embarrassed because "political equality . . . is likely to be sooner achieved in Mississippi than in Illinois."

Southerners claimed that Republicans used the freedmen to keep the Republican party in power. They pointed out that most northern states did not allow blacks to vote. Stung by this charge, Republican congressmen prepared yet another amendment to the Constitution. The amendment, the Fifteenth, guaranteed all men the right to vote. By summer 1870, the Fifteenth Amendment had been added to the Constitution. (Women did not receive the right to vote until 1920, when the Nineteenth Amendment was passed). By accepting the Fifteenth Amendment, the last Confederate states—Virginia, Georgia, Mississippi, and Texas—rejoined the Union.

Members of the Ku Klux Klan attack a black family in their home.

But the situation in the South worsened. The KKK stepped up its attacks against both white and black Republicans. Alarmed, President Grant signed several acts into law. The acts allowed Union soldiers to hunt down groups of the Klan and arrest them. During the early 1870s, the soldiers attempted to carry out their orders. In some southern states, black soldiers were organized into military units. Bloody clashes occurred between southern whites and Union troops. Startled by these reports, Grant worried that the South could explode into warfare between the races. Worse, he feared that the nation was drifting back into civil war.

President Grant turned to Congress for help.

But by the mid-1870s, ten years after the end of the Civil War, Northerners had grown weary of the freedmen and their problems. They believed that the Thirteenth, Fourteenth, and Fifteenth Amendments were enough to protect black civil rights throughout the country. Neither Grant nor Congress wanted to risk further violence by sending more Union soldiers into the South. In addition, Grant's administration suffered from scandals and reports of corruption. As a result, the credibility of the Republicans was severely damaged.

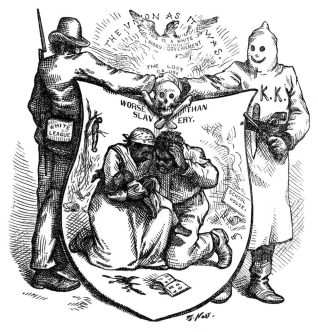

By the 1870s, illustrations such as this depicted the condition of blacks in the South, who were oppressed by both the white-run government and the Ku Klux Klan, as worse than slavery.

As support for Reconstruction faded, southern states gradually fell back under white control. Whites used violence to keep blacks from voting and from holding office. White and black Republican leaders were harassed and attacked until they were driven from the South. By the 1876 presidential election, only three southern states still had Republican governments. The Republicans nominated a Civil War hero, Rutherford B. Hayes, for president. The Democrats nominated Samuel Tilden. Both men were known for their honesty and strength of character.

Rutherford B. Hayes (top) and Samuel J. Tilden

When the election results were counted, Tilden received 250,000 more votes than Hayes. But presidential elections are decided by electoral votes, not individual votes. Each state, depending on the size of its population, has a number of electoral votes. The candidate with the most votes in a state wins all of its electoral votes. The candidate with the most electoral votes then wins the election. Sometimes, the candidate with the most votes in the nation does not win in many individual states. This happened in 1876. Tilden did not have enough electoral votes. In fact, Hayes had won the election by votes from the three southern states that were still under Republican control. The Democrats protested, claiming that the votes from the three states had been falsely counted.

The nation was thrown into a crisis. Some citizens worried that the country would suffer another civil war. Finally, in March 1877, the Compromise of 1877 was reached. The Democrats would allow Hayes to become president if he promised to withdraw the last Union troops from the South. Hayes agreed. Without Union soldiers to enforce the law, Reconstruction was over. The freedmen were left to fight for themselves.

Reconstruction is considered by many to be one of the boldest experiments in American history. For a few brief years, the Radical

Republicans tried to make the United States a land where all men were created equal. To achieve this goal, they gave the federal government the power to protect every American citizen's civil rights. Their Reconstruction was a failure. When Union soldiers left the South, blacks were left unprotected. During the next fifty years, their rights would be stripped from them by white-controlled governments. Blacks would endure racism, poverty, and segregated (separate) schools. But in the 1950s, a new generation of blacks would use the Thirteenth, Fourteenth, and Fifteenth Amendments to renew their demands for civil rights. A new struggle for equality would seize the attention of the nation. However, this struggle is not yet complete. Today, the United States continues to work to provide equality and freedom to all its citizens.

This 1875 illustration expresses the fear of the violence against blacks that would follow the removal of federal troops from the South.

GLOSSARY

carpetbagger

Ku Klux Klan member

abolish – to put an end to something officially

Black Codes – laws passed by white southerners in an effort to return blacks to a state of slavery

carpetbaggers – name given to northerners who became leaders in the South during Reconstruction

civil rights – a citizen's rights, including the right to vote, to assemble, and to receive the protection of the law

congressional Reconstruction – the program of Reconstruction that was controlled by Congress

credibility – believability

gulf – difference between people

Ku Klux Klan – an organization of whites that used violence and terror to keep blacks from gaining political control in the South

plantation – large farm that usually specializes in growing one crop

presidential Reconstruction – the program of Reconstruction that was controlled by the president

Radical Republicans – a group of Republican congressmen who urged a revolutionary plan of Reconstruction

reconstruct – to rebuild something that has been destroyed

traitor – person who betrays his or her country

veto – the right or power of a president to reject a bill that has been passed by a legislature and to keep it from becoming law

TIMELINE

March: Seceding
Southern states form
the Confederacy

April: Civil War begins

1860 *November:* Abraham Lincoln
elected president

1861

1862 Lincoln begins plan for Reconstruction

1863 Lincoln issues Emancipation Proclamation

1865

1866

1867

1868

1869

1877 *March:* Compromise of 1877

February:
Johnson vetoes
Freedmen's Bill

March:
Congress passes
Civil Rights Act

June: Congress
passes 14th
Amendment

March: Congress passes
First Reconstruction Act

February:
Congress
passes 15th
Amendment

March: Congress establishes
Freedmen's Bureau

April 9: Civil War ends

April 14: Lincoln assassinated;
Andrew Johnson becomes
president

April – December: Johnson's
plan for Reconstruction

December: Congress refuses to
seat southern representatives

May: Johnson survives
impeachment by one vote

November: Ulysses S.
Grant elected president

INDEX *(Boldface page numbers indicate illustrations.)*

PHOTO CREDITS

Photographs ©: AP/Wide World Photos: 8; Archive Photos: 19 (American Stock), 5, 6, 7, 10, 17, 25, 28, 31 left; Corbis-Bettmann: 2, 9, 14, 21, 24, 30 top, 31 right; North Wind Picture Archives: cover, 1, 3, 15, 16, 22, 26, 27; Rufus and Willard Saxton Papers, Manuscripts & Archives, Yale University Library: 20; Rutherford B. Hayes Presidential Center: 23, 30 bottom; Stock Montage, Inc.: 11, 12, 29; The Museum of the Confederacy: 13; maps: TJS Design.

ABOUT THE AUTHOR

Brendan January was born and raised in Pleasantville, New York. He earned his B.A. in history and English at Haverford College and an M.A. in Journalism from Columbia University. An American history enthusiast, he has written several books for Children's Press, including *The Emancipation Proclamation, Fort Sumter, The Dred Scott Decision, The Lincoln-Douglas Debates,* and *The Assassination of Abraham Lincoln* (Cornerstones of Freedom). Mr. January lives in New York City.